T0198961

HERE IN
SPIRIT

Answers to Common Questions My Clients Ask of
Their Loved Ones on the Other Side

CHERYL PILLAR, THE DC MEDIUM

Balboa Press books may be ordered through booksellers or by contacting:

Balboa Press
A Division of Hay House
1663 Liberty Drive
Bloomington, IN 47403
www.balboapress.com
1 (877) 407-4847

ISBN: 978-1-9822-4572-6 (sc)
ISBN: 978-1-9822-4571-9 (e)

Print information available on the last page.

Balboa Press rev. date: 04/14/2020

BALBOA.PRESS
A DIVISION OF HAY HOUSE

Here in Spirit

Answers to common questions my clients ask
of their loved ones on the Other Side

Cheryl Pillar
The DC Medium

When I look at the northern lights…I see our ancestors dancing around a sacred fire, lighting the way for us when it's time for us to cross over from this physical world and join them.

Molly Larkin, "What do the Northern Lights mean for us?"

DEDICATION

For my Mom and Dad. Thank you for your love, guidance, and support.

Dad, your guidance is still felt and your love still surrounds us all!

To my clients. Thank you for allowing me to connect with your loved ones and bring through healing messages. I'm very grateful to those who opened themselves up and shared their experiences so others may find clarity and closure.

To Fiona Adams, my best friend who encouraged me to pursue my talents!

INTRODUCTION

By way of introductions, I'm Cheryl Pillar, the DC Medium and owner of SoulConX. This is my first book (exciting!). You haven't seen me on TV or likely anywhere else, but this book isn't about me, so I'll keep this part really short. Just a little background so you know I'm speaking from experience might be helpful.

Most psychic mediums can attest to the fact that the gift comes to light in young children. I wasn't always able to validate the visitations and messages I was receiving - I wasn't going to walk up to a random stranger and say "Hey, your Grandmother's here and has a message for you." Yah, that might not be received well. I did have several experiences I was able to validate. My turning point was when I was in Yoga class. My Nana appeared and at that moment, I knew. She had just died. In a calm panic, I finished class and went to my car. My phone was already ringing. It was my Dad. I answered the phone

"Nana died."

"Yes, how did you know," he questioned.

"She visited me in Yoga class at 9:08."

He paused, "That's the MINUTE she died."

I told my friend Fiona about my experience and she encouraged me to take a class. (I had no idea they had classes for this stuff!)

HOW TO READ THIS BOOK

Since completing my psychic mediumship training, I've conducted thousands of readings. I started to notice a pattern: most people asked very similar questions. I'd like to share what I learned from spirit along with some short client stories to represent how they may show up. Of note, these are MY experiences and beliefs based on what spirit has shown ME. This book is a way to share some of the heartfelt insights I've gained through my readings over the years.

A little bit about the structure of the book will help you follow along. There are 4 pages in each section.

1. The first page is the answer to my the frequently asked question my clients ask of their loved ones who have passed. In the first section, generally clients as "is my loved one ok?": What you'll see on the page is spirit's answer "I'm ok."

2. The second page is in my experience, a summary of what I've learned from spirit.

3. The third page is a picture of my client and their loved one in spirit or something that is meaningful to them.

4. The fourth page with the quotes is an example of a client's story about their loved one, touching points from their reading, and the clarity and closure they received to help them heal.

You may have obtained this book to help yourself heal or from a family or friend as a sympathy book to help lift your spirits during a difficult time! Either way, this book has found itself in your hands for a reason.

" I'm ok "

4

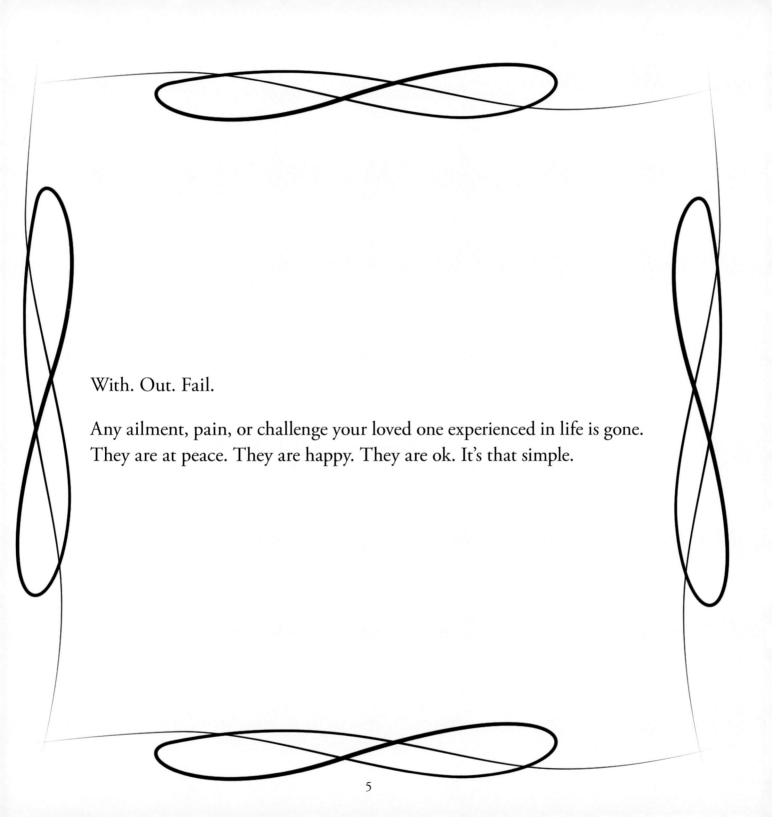

With. Out. Fail.

Any ailment, pain, or challenge your loved one experienced in life is gone. They are at peace. They are happy. They are ok. It's that simple.

Nicole L.'s Story

My sister Christine, her husband, and two children were hit head on by a tractor-trailer in 2017 and passed immediately at the scene. I feel them around me and have experienced actual touches to my shoulders when no one is there.

During my reading, Christine said she knew our parents recently moved; that the house was much more suited to our parent's lifestyle. Mom and Christine enjoyed home design, yet their styles were somewhat different. When Christine commented she did not like a particular color Mom used in the new house, I knew it was her 100%.

To know she is ok in the afterlife and that the whole family is together has brought me much needed peace. Having these moments with them again has helped with the gut-wrenching grief and being greeted now with each reading with my niece dancing in, is well, a very comforting feeling and makes me smile.

"

I'm proud of you

"

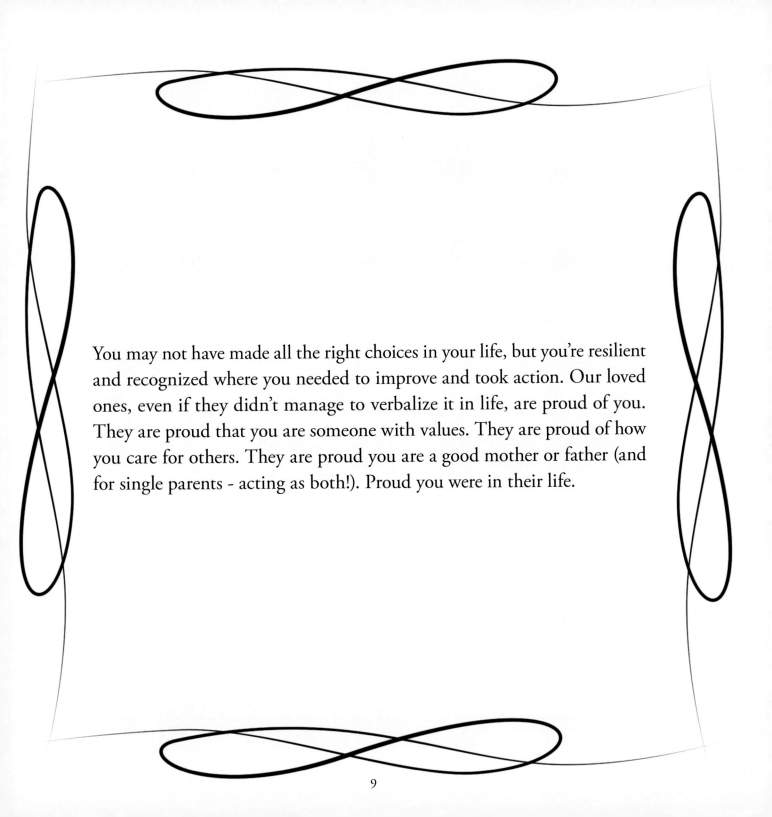

You may not have made all the right choices in your life, but you're resilient and recognized where you needed to improve and took action. Our loved ones, even if they didn't manage to verbalize it in life, are proud of you. They are proud that you are someone with values. They are proud of how you care for others. They are proud you are a good mother or father (and for single parents - acting as both!). Proud you were in their life.

Me and my
sweet dad

Amy K.'s Story

My father George died in my arms. I was completely heartbroken, overcome with grief, and wasn't functioning.

The message from my dad that meant the most to me, was that he was proud of me. I had made a lot of mistakes and finally was a point in my life where I would consider myself successful. I tried so hard to show my dad I've improved my life so he would be proud.

Knowing he is proud of me - seeing where I was and how hard I worked to improve - and who I've become fills my heart! It motivates me to continue to be a daughter he will always be proud of, instead of falling deep in a depression hole and not trying anymore. After my reading, I smiled more, embraced happiness again!

"

All souls go to heaven

"

This is very different than what some religions teach. Suicides. Gang bangers. Some people would expect they end up in hell. That's what we are taught.

It's just not what I've been shown by spirit. God forgives and allows our souls another chance.

With suicides for example, they are getting a reset, per se. A mulligan. A gang banger is able to view his/her life and how it impacted others (think 6 degrees of separation from Kevin Bacon) and see how they can be a better person in the next life.

We all get another shot; over and over again until we get it right. Our loved ones heal from this life and continue to learn and understand, enabling them to grow and be ready for their next life.

Nicole W.'s Story

My brother Matt and I were so close. We had a rough upbringing and were able to support each other as children and into adulthood. Matt internalized his emotions and didn't want people to know he struggled. He was witty and fun and if you didn't know he struggled with depression you wouldn't know. To the shock of family and friends, he took his life at age 32.

The message he gave me was "It had to be. I needed to reset." That resonated with me as I know we are on our own life journey and this was part of his.

My body honestly feels "lighter" since I was able to communicate with my brother Matt. Hearing him joke about peanut butter and jelly sandwiches and fishing with Grandpa allowed me to see that just because he has passed away doesn't mean that when I talk to him in my mind I don't need to be so serious. Since his passing, my communication with him was always with a heavy heart and undo seriousness. His jokey manner during our session made me realize that I can still be silly and light-hearted when I reach out to him. The comfort, closure, and reassurance from knowing Matt is in heaven is immeasurable!

"
Sorry,
not sorry
"

Your loved ones have gone through a life review. They see how what they did impacted you throughout your life and today. They see how their actions affected your behavior and moods - and how yours affected others.

After seeing all this, are they sorry?

Generally, yes! They see that and want to express their sincere apologies for their behavior and how they hurt you. On rare occasion, they may not take responsibility for their actions and indicate that your feelings and actions are yours alone. Sigh, a lesson for their next life.

They also may not be sorry because that was the lesson they were SUPPOSED to learn in this life and the lesson YOU were SUPPOSED to learn. While it was a tough pill to swallow - it was what our souls decided before coming to this earth and therefore, nothing to be sorry about.

Sophie J.'s Story

My dad, Stanley, was a psychologist and incredibly complicated. He loved us deeply, but he was not always truthful, even about innocuous things that were easy to dispute. Our small family of my mom, younger brother and I used that to our advantage and he became the scapegoat for our family. That said, we always knew he loved us.

When he came through in our reading, he mentioned his "banana nose." He was very good looking and had a rather large, Greek nose. In the cartoon, "Charlie Brown," Snoopy received an award "banana nose dog of the year" and that's how Dad got his nickname.

He acknowledged his lack of transparency and honesty (albeit not really apologetically) but understood the impact he had on us. And we had the opportunity to tell him how much we really did love him as well. Knowing he could still joke with us about his "banana nose" showed us while he isn't perfect, he is still dad and always will be.

" I have a new "life" "

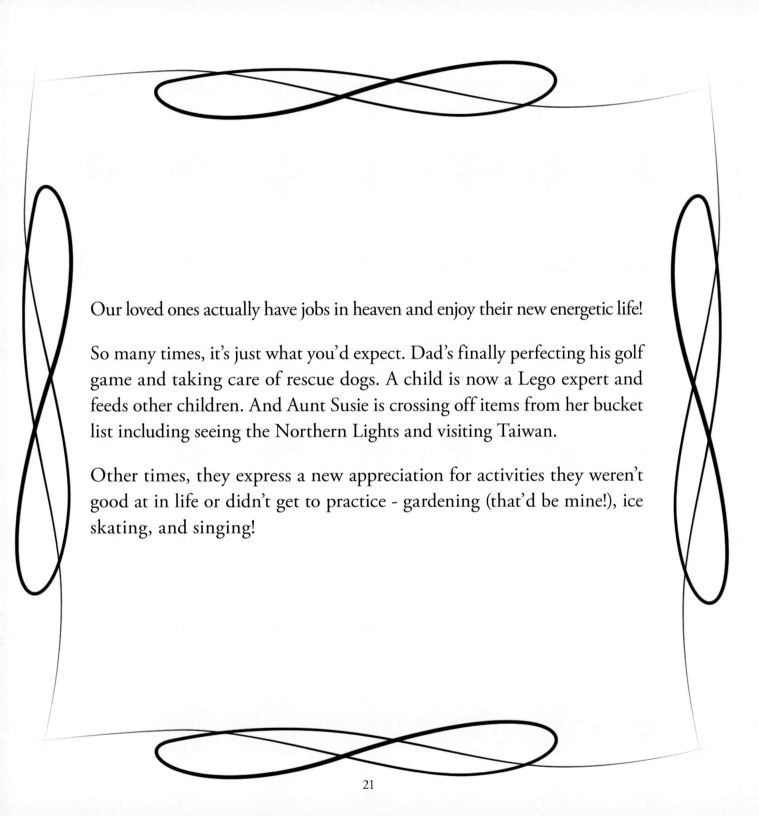

Our loved ones actually have jobs in heaven and enjoy their new energetic life!

So many times, it's just what you'd expect. Dad's finally perfecting his golf game and taking care of rescue dogs. A child is now a Lego expert and feeds other children. And Aunt Susie is crossing off items from her bucket list including seeing the Northern Lights and visiting Taiwan.

Other times, they express a new appreciation for activities they weren't good at in life or didn't get to practice - gardening (that'd be mine!), ice skating, and singing!

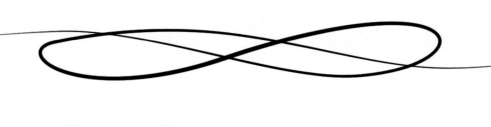

Ottamissiah (Missy) M.'s Story

During my reading, my son Demitrice told me he had an amazing job in heaven; he is responsible for making parts of the world into art! It was the perfect assignment for him because he was a brilliant artist.

A few months after he gave me this message, I was on a plane to Alaska. As the plane came in for a landing, I looked out the window. I knew I saw some of my son's work! I had never experienced mountains with a beautiful purple hue surrounded in clouds and frost. With tears flowing I whispered "I see you Demitrice! Mom sees you!"

"

I see you and send you signs

"

Your loved ones come to you in a variety of ways after they pass. Unfortunately, we're all naturally skeptical – so we tend to brush off the signs and are dismissive as "wishful thinking." They are still around, send signs, communicate, and watch you (not in a creepy way!). Please pay attention and trust whatever sign you do receive.

Treat it like a conversation as if your loved one is right there in the flesh. They hear you. They talk to you. They see what's going on and help you get through your everyday life. You can feel their presence, hear them like a voice in your head, or witness a sign. It could be a song on the radio that reminds you of them. An item moved from its typical spot (so mischievous!). Or a coin or feather out of place.

The signs may not be as overt as you would like but they're there. They need you to acknowledge their presence as much as you want to believe it's really them. Smile and say "thank you, I know it was you!"

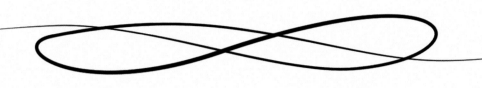

Kristen H.'s Story

My grandfather, Dallas, passed away and indicated he sends me signs in the form of angels.

I had planted a tree in front of his house for my friend Sabrina after she died. I transplanted Sabrina's tree and other flowers from his yard to mine to create a memory garden that I can view from my kitchen window.

While I was digging a hole in the backyard with my hand shovel, I hit a small plastic angel six inches deep. Sending me an angel is a very big sign which gave me comfort to know he's still around watching over me - like an angel.

"

I'm surrounded by family and friends that passed before me

"

The whole "famn damily" (my Nana's way she said "damn family") is here (whether welcome or not!).

Our loved ones were met with open arms in Heaven by someone that is comforting.

They spend time with family and friends that they knew, as well as those from other lives. Our loved ones want us to know "I'm comfortable and surrounded by love!"

Shirley Q.'s Story

My fiancé, Craig and I lost our daughter. A few years later, Craig was in the wrong place at the wrong time and was shot in the head - dying instantly. This hurt my heart more than anything knowing not only my daughter was gone, but also the love of my life was gone too.

During my reading, Craig mentioned that Raquel greeted him when he crossed which helped him transition in a peaceful way.

This kept me calm and it made me feel at peace knowing that they are at peace and spending the time together in heaven that they didn't get on earth. I now have hope and faith that I will also be okay.

"

Grief is real

"

I know reading this book might bring some clarity and closure, yet you do still need to grieve. It's a necessary healing process. And it's not fun. Heck, it's downright hard. It sucks. I've heard from some of my clients that they miss their loved one SO much that they want to join them in heaven. Your loved one is still here with you – in another way. It's not the same, I know. If you feel that way know three things (1) taking your life is a permanent solution to a temporary problem, (2) the way you feel about your loved one who passed is the way your family and friends would feel about you if you also passed, and (3) help is available. Reach out to your friends and family, join a support group, or call:

National Suicide Prevention Lifeline 1-800-273-8255

THE STORY CONTINUES

After I've answered some of your questions about your loved ones, you may ask "Why bother going to a medium?"

Because you want to know that YOUR loved one is OK. That YOUR loved one is with family. That things are resolved with YOUR loved one and the nuances of your relationship.

How has a reading helped you gain clarity and closure? How did it affect you?

Let's continue the conversation to help others heal! Share your story on FaceBook @dcmedium or directly with Cheryl at www.dcmedium.com.

CONNECT WITH THE DC MEDIUM

Cheryl Pillar is the DC Medium and founder of SoulConX. She "came out" as a psychic medium to her family and friends in 2014. Cheryl is a single mother, CPA and a professional consultant by day, so you can imagine, right? Not really the eclectic medium-type! She knew spirit was around since she was a small child. Cheryl was able to feel when her loved ones were ill or in danger, knew when they had been injured or passed, and felt them in spirit. Her guides encouraged her for years to write a book to share insights from spirits and healing words from her clients. Cheryl lives in Fairfax, VA with her son Collin, daughter Emma, and springer spaniel, Lily.

Look for Cheryl Pillar on Facebook @dcmedium or her website www.dcmedium.com

Printed in the United States
By Bookmasters